"THERE IS NOTHING WRONG WITH A GOOD GIRL HAVING A NAUGHTY SIDE."

-A good girl with a naughty side

HOOD BITCH, GOOD PUSSY, I AIN'T AVERAGE

Nails done, hair done, ass too

I WALK AND I TALK LIKE A HOE 'CAUSE I AM

BADASS BITCH, BAD ATTITUDE

PUSSY SWEET, PUSSY TIGHT

CHOKE ME, SPANK ME, LOOK AT ME, THANK ME

Feelin' like a pornstar

k. I'm done. I need your cock!

LOOK IN MY EYES AND FUCK MY MOUTH

I SPIT, I SLURP, I DO THE JOB RIGHT.

I DON'T COOK
I DON'T CLEAN
I'M A
BLOWJOB
QUEEN

I know how to suck and I know how to fuck

WINE ME,
DINE ME,
69 ME.

Grab my hair and fuck me like a dog

FUCK ME AND CALL ME A GOOD GIRL

HARDER!

Ride me like you stole me!

Fuck it! Carpe diem.

JUST LIKE THAT!

DEEPER, DEEPER, I NEED A REAPER

GRAB MY TITS!

FUCK THIS WAP!

MAKE MY PUSSY RAIN, BABYY!

Spread my legs not the virus!

HOLY SHIT, I'M CUMMING!

MAKE IT CREAM, MAKE ME SCREAM!

I love being your fuck slut.

PAINT MY FACE!

You like that baby?

MMMMMM, YOU TASTE SO GOOD.

Made in the USA
Columbia, SC
15 November 2024